Simplifying the Scientific Writing

ISBN: 978-1-7779034-1-1

Written & Edited by:
Dr. M. Irfan-Maqsood, Ph.D.

ISBN: 978-1-7779034-1-1

Simplifying the Scientific Writing

(Learn the Basics! Book Series)

ISBN: 978-1-7779034-1-1

© 2023- by M. Irfan-maqsood & IMAQPRESS

Bookstore Price: 12 $ / 20 ₼ / 10 £ / 11€

Published on April, 2023

ISBN: 978-1-7779034-1-1

Published by **IMAQPRESS Inc.**
800-136 Market Ave
Winnipeg, Manitoba
Canada, R3B 0P4
www.imaqpress.com
info@imaqpress.com

ISBN: 978-1-7779034-1-1

TABLE OF CONTENTS

ISBN: 978-1-7779034-1-1

Preface

Since the ancient times, human beings started communications, they developed techniques to write on stones and then papers. Very few were in any society doing the job as writer and they were considered the most secretive and knowledgeable people. Scientific writing / editing is one of the three basic pillars of an academic career along with the teaching/education and doing research/lab work. If you want to have an impactful career in Academia or research industry, it is impossible to have it without being skilled enough in scientific writing, editing and publishing. Scientific writing / editing is a multidisciplinary career of integrative skills and knowledge. Simplifying the Scientific Writing as a part of Learn the Basics! Book series of IMAQPRESS is all-in-one collection of knowledge and tips to step into the scientific writing and editing career.

Simplifying the Scientific Writing
ISBN: 978-1-7779034-1-1

ISBN: 978-1-7779034-1-1

Chapter 1:

Introduction to Scientific Writing & Scientific Publishing

Science has been defined as the research mechanism/process of generating and managing the knowledge in the form of testable conclusions, theories or laws. Science is one of the three main pillars of academic career and is the most vital part of it especially when it is compared with the education or policy making/management. Science could be classified into two general following categories;,

1- Science Inside the Lab
2- Science Outside the Lab

Science Inside the Lab (wet or dry lab) is the most common type of science in our surrounding where scientists or researchers are working to conduct the experiments using some equipment, materials or methodologies for the purpose of generating knowledge in the form of testable conclusions, theories or laws. The concept of dry labs is a novel concept of using informatics approaches and data analytical tools to generate the strong knowledge. Whereas, generating knowledge using public opinions, studying cases, conclusion of an analytic or technical reports etc comes under the cetagory of *Science Outside the Lab (SOtL)*. SOtL is aimed to explore the relationships of science, innovation, policy, and societal outcomes before it is being stored or applied in society. Ethics in science and scientific policies are famous sections of SOtL.

ISBN: 978-1-7779034-1-1

The significance of science outside the lab is undeniable because it helps the decision-making in the government and businesses at the local, state, federal, and international levels to keep the flow of funding and public trust smoothly. Science is seen by the productivity it has in the form of **scientific articles or papers** as novel pieces of knowledge which are very specific types of scholarly publications following a unique set of protocols and formats of editing and peer-reviewing. Scientific publications are scholarly articles published by students, scholars, researchers or any other member of the scientific communities in the peer-reviewed scholarly journals. Following are some famous types of Scientific articles;

1. *Original research papers*

2. *Literature review papers*

3. *Research notes/reports*

4. *Clinical case studies or Epidemiological reports*

5. *Scientific letters/commentaries/opinions*

6. *Scientific hypothesis or ideas*

7. *Scientific policy reports*

8. *Technology development reports etc.*

ISBN: 978-1-7779034-1-1

These scientific articles are then distributed among the society and transformed into simple language for the general public in the form of **science contents / science texts** as a part of **science journalism** which are written to deliver the science in the form of;

1. *Science/research news*

2. *Science blog posts*

3. *Scientific/academic announcements,*

4. *Science updates*

5. *Science editorials etc.*

Both together, the scientific articles or papers and the scientific contents or texts are known as **Scientific Writing**.

Scientific / Academic Publishing

Scientific or academic publishing is the process of distribution of academic outputs e.g. research, reviews, opinions, perspectives etc which are being published in the form of scientific article or papers or in some cases as an academic book or technological patent, either as a part of an independent project or a graduate degree thesis project at the university lab or a research institute.

ISBN: 978-1-7779034-1-1

Peer-reviewed scholarly journals are nationally or internationally reputed scientific journals which are well respected among the scientific communities because of their **authenticity** in **editorial board**, **information** and **research** they are providing on a specific discipline.

Following are the top 10 scholar journals in the world based on their impact factor - 2021 (IF-2021), a globally recognized parameter for the journal quality assigned by **Web of Science (WoS)** in their annual **Journal Citation Report (JCR)** managed and published by **Institute of Scientific Information (ISI)** by *Clarivate Analytic*;

1. *CA- A Cancer Journal for Clinicians | 286 IF*
2. *Natural Review Materials | 124 IF*
3. *Reviews of Modern Physics | 76 IF*
4. *Nature Reviews Genetics | 74 IF*
5. *New England Journal of Medicine | 66 IF*
6. *Cell | 59 IF*
7. *Energy and Environmental Sciences | 56 IF*
8. *Living Reviews in Relativity | 54 IF*
9. *Annual Review of Psychology | 38 IF*
10. *Quarterly Journal of Economics | 23 IF*

ISBN: 978-1-7779034-1-1

All peer-reviewed scholarly journals are equipped with some special software and tools known as **journal management systems (JMS)** to ease the publishing process, maximizing the online visibility and to receive high citations following different kind of peer-review process involving the researchers and academics around the world to evaluate the scientific contents on voluntary basis and then after being accepted these articles are published online in several formats such as PDF, HTML, XML, RSS etc so that search engines i.e. Google, Yahoo, MSN etc can crawl these articles for global visibility and citations count. **ScholarOne™** is the world's most attractive journal management system introduced by Thomson Reuters followed by the **author2reader™**, **Editorial Manager™** and freely available **Open Journal System (OJS)**.

Article Review and Publishing Process

When you have decided to publish your article, it means you have something important to Such as an interesting new result or conclusion to report to the scientific community. Once you've decided to publish your article, visit the journal website and go through its old issues to get a sense of the journal's style and formatting protocol so you can format your article accordingly.

ISBN: 978-1-7779034-1-1

Usually, journals have special pages for authors explaining their submission and publishing policies. You should also know the journal peer-review process, which is for,

1. *To filter what is published as "science".*
2. *To provide researchers with a perspective.*

When a paper is written and formatted as per journal submission policies, it is ready to be submitted for evaluation. Almost all journals have two phased review process (*1- editorial review and 2- peer-review*) to evaluate the quality of an article submitted to their journals. Editorial review is the process of reviewing and analysing the article by the editorial board members or editorial management team of the journal.

This first phase of review is usually to analyse that either journal wants to proceed for the further efforts or want to reject because there is nothing interesting for them which should be called a **science**. Normally, this first review process is to analyse the format of an article and to evaluate that author/s has/have followed the journal submission and publishing policies. If the paper is not rejected within first or two weeks after submission, its mean the journal management team has forwarded the article for peer-review process.

ISBN: 978-1-7779034-1-1

Peer review is a process of obtaining opinions from the relevant experts regarding the methodologies applied, logics on scientific conclusion and the statement being published in the paper. There is several types of peer-review process a journal can adopt such as;

1- ***Blind peer-review***

2- ***Open peer-review***

3- ***Collaborative peer-review***

Following schematic diagram describes the whole process of scientific publishing;

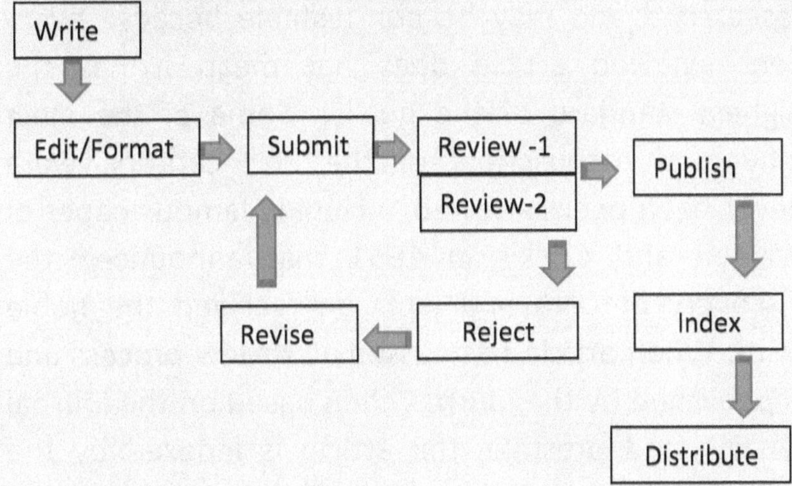

Article Review and Publishing Process

ISBN: 978-1-7779034-1-1

In **blind peer-review process**, identities of one or both (author/s or reviewer/s) are hidden and could be called as *single* or *double blind peer-review process*, respectively whereas in **open peer-review process**, identities of both are *revealed* to each other. **Collaborative peer-review process** is a very unique process applied by many journals in which the editorial board and author discuss to select the subject related and specified reviewers and request them to evaluate the paper and help the both (editors and authors) to *improve the quality of paper*. It is important to remember that a paper accepted in peer review can still be poorly written and poorly researched and may be non-testable because every peer-reviewed article does not mean it has the highest standard of the quality. Some of the most influential manuscripts of the 20th century, were never been peer reviewed, including famous paper of Watson and Crick's in 1951 that announced the discovery of DNA and later on received the noble prize. When article has passed all review process and is published by the journal, then based on the journal ranking and prestige, the article is indexed by the indexing databases and then distributed for global visibility to receive the response from the global scientific community in the form of citations etc.

ISBN: 978-1-7779034-1-1

Scientific Indexing Databases

Almost all senior academics are well aware about the scientific indexing and ranking systems such as Google Scholar, Scopus, CABI, ISI, PubMed and Impact factors (average citations per document), h-index etc, respectively. All scholarly academic journals should be indexed by an indexing database. There are following three types of journal indexing databases which tells the authenticity of the journal as per their metrics;

1. *General Indexing Databases*
2. *Subject Specific Indexing Databases*
3. *Journal Ranking Databases*

General Indexing Databases are only for the purpose of global visibility and these databases retrieve data regarding the key performing indexes from other prestigious indexing databases. Google Scholar is an example of general indexing databases. Subject specific prestigious indexing databases are nationally and internationally approved and accredited databases for the scholarly journals. These databases have some rigorous evaluation criteria before they index the journals.

ISBN: 978-1-7779034-1-1

PubMed for medical and life sciences, **CAB International** for agriculture sciences, **IEEE** for engineering sciences etc, are some examples of subject specific prestigious indexing databases. If you are publishing in a journal which is indexed by its own subject specific prestigious databases, then it is ok to publish in that journal because that journal meets the basic criteria to be called a prestigious international scholarly journal.

Journal Ranking Databases are the most reputed and authentic indexing databases because they set the parameters for the standardization and grading of the quality of a journal and they regularly update the ranking of a journal every year to clarify the efficiency and progress of that journal each year. **Web of Science (WoS)** and **Scopus** are the two only prestigious journal ranking databases because both assign an indexing number and rank the journal in their reports.

Impact factor is a scientometric index calculated by Clarivate Analytics and published in the annual JCR (journal citation report) of ISI-WoS whereas **SCImago Journal Rank or SJR** is a scientometric index published by Scopus, an Elsevier's abstract and citation database.

ISBN: 978-1-7779034-1-1

ISI-WoS (Web of Science)

Institute of Science Information (ISI) as a part of Clarivate Analytics and formerly owned by Thomson Reuter holdings manages the WoS and evaluates the academic journals every year and rank the journals based on their ranking criteria, i.e. Impact Factor (IF) and publish the journal citations report (JCR) of all evaluated journals each year. IF and JCR were started in 1974 and are enlisting the approximately 12000 most prestigious journals of the world every year. This is the most acceptable ranking of journals as the journals are being ranked on the average citations received by the journal's article.

Scopus-Elsevier

Scopus is Elsevier's abstract and citation database launched in 2004. Scopus covers nearly 36,377 titles (22,794 active titles and 13,583 Inactive titles) from approximately 12,000 publishers, of which 34,346 are peer-reviewed journals in top-level subject fields: life sciences, social sciences, physical sciences and health sciences. Scopus, along with citations, also counts some other factors such as regularity etc when evaluates the journals for selection to index in their database.

ISBN: 978-1-7779034-1-1

Scientific Citations are the abbreviated alphanumeric expression embedded in the body of a scientific publication describing bibliographic references at the end of a publications for the purpose of acknowledging the scientific works. Scientific citations received by a research paper indicate how useful a scholarly article is rather than just a piece of useless knowledge. Scientific citations are the important figures when research quality of an academic expert is evaluated because these figures tell us how the useful knowledge that scientists have produced as the productivity of science during their academic career. Journal citations are the referenced bibliography of the articles published in that journal as it tells the value of science published in the journal. The **impact factor (IF)** or **journal impact factor (JIF)** of an academic journal is a measure reflecting the yearly average number of citations to recent articles published in that journal. This is worth mentioning that highest impact factor of a journal is 286 (2022) belongs to *CA: A Cancer Journal for Clinicians* published by American Cancer Society indicating the standards and professionalism in the presentation of science to the global community.

ISBN: 978-1-7779034-1-1

Chapter 2:

Required Skills and Tools in Scientific Writing

Career in research and academia is a career benefiting many aspects of global society such as providing solutions to social, cultural, economic and health issues based on the scientific and technological knowledge. Whenever there was a crises for humanity, the experts from academia with the support of industry found the solutions to tackle the issues. The most obvious example is the just passed Covid-19 pandemic which has been tackled by the joint efforts of academia and industry. When it comes to the professionalism in academia or research career, writing and editing skills are the pre-requisites. For example, writing a cover letter and career objective for your resume is the first and most important text written at the start of your career. Writing and editing the official reports, writing the summaries to justify your actions and activities in the organization you are working for, are the weekly cycles of your professional life. It is a fact that you will not be able to sustain your job if you are not skilled enough in writing and editing.

Must Require Skill in Scientific Writing

Scientific writing is a major skill or set of skills required many minor but important skills. Scientific writing along with editing/publishing skills, are all you need to establish a career in research or academia.

ISBN: 978-1-7779034-1-1

The most important and must require skill in scientific writing is the ability to create a story from raw data or an imagination because a scientific paper is a story, the more interesting it is, the more audience it will have and more audience means more readership and more citations which will enhance the impact of your research at international level.

Creativity is the base of writing because a writer is a creator, a creator of stories from a scratch or a raw data. Story creation needs the deep imagination power because more you can imagine deeply about a topic; more comprehensive story you can create. Developing the skills of story creation is a trial-error-improved kind of set of skills where you learn the important points in the story creation because when readers and reviewers found the blind spots of your story, they either can improve your story with valuable suggestions or they can destroy your reputation by adding bad reviews. Basic knowledge of scientific writing and important components of a scientific article is the backbone of conceptualization of creativity because you can understand the what to create and how to create?

*The purpose of this book, **"simplifying the Scientific Writing: Learn the Basic!"** is the summarization of basic concepts in scientific writing, editing and publishing process to improve your scientific or academic writing skills.*

ISBN: 978-1-7779034-1-1

Creating a story or conceptualizing it does not require the set of hundred pages' text. All you need is to just summarize the story in your brain before even the start of writing. On early stages, you may forget the concepts of story but don't worry, don't start writing until the concepts are clear and very strong in your mind. When you reach this level, then start mapping the concepts because it will help you to find the blind spots or flaws f your story concepts. You have to find the minimum 10 blind spots or flaws in your own concept map and then start writing the abstracts and then finalize the first draft of your scientific article or a book.

A scientific article or a book is not just a sum of text and references, it is a unique explanation of what has had happened, or what is happening or what is going to happen in near future based on the scientific facts or mythical concepts (in case of a book). If you succeeded to understand and create such a statement and have learnt how to justify your statements using references, facts and figures, then draft of your scientific paper or book is ready for editing and publishing. There are several common mistakes performed by an early career researcher or author which you can find here and can avoid in your writing.

ISBN: 978-1-7779034-1-1

Common Mistakes in Writing a Scientific Paper

When it comes to write a scientific paper, almost every young researcher has drafted his/her first paper but several common mistakes are usual, for example...

1. *They focus on data instead of analysing data*
2. *They assemble the text instead of assembling knowledge*
3. *Their draft has not been edited by senior researchers*

In many cases, the main issue is not the text or references, but a creative story having a perfect concept. Consider the example of a mountain full of stones as a draft of your paper, and use your skills to transform these stones into valuable gems.

Remember following key points before or while drafting your article or book;

1. *You should have enough useful content with references*
2. *You should know how to correlate incidences of history (especially in case of a book)*
3. *You should know how to write a Critique and do Data Analysis*
4. *You should know how to create consistency in sentences*
5. *You should know basic marketing strategies*
6. *Writing science has no paid vacations and benefits*

ISBN: 978-1-7779034-1-1

Basic Abilities to Write a Scientific Paper:

Writing skills required strong grip over grammar and vocabulary because strong knowledge of **grammar** and **vocabulary** helps you to **structure** a wonderful piece of knowledge with beautiful sentences at the highest level of **accuracy** and **clarity**. To assemble several pieces of knowledge to create a big story and to create a **cohesion** and **coherence** of knowledge in all sections of your story, an author should develop following basic abilities to produce and correlate enough texts to write and finalize a scientific paper or a book. There are several ways to enhance the writing skills and abilities to create stories, discussed in following pages.

1. *Ability to Select (Ideas and Contents)*

2. *Ability to Understand Scientific Methods (How Science Works?)*

3. *Ability to Evaluate (Research Done by Scientists)*

4. *Ability to Correlate the Authentic Results*

5. *Ability to Make Conclusion & Suggestions*

ISBN: 978-1-7779034-1-1

How to Acquire the Writing-Editing Skills?

First of all, be a part of volunteer teams of student's scientific magazines published by your university and ask the editorial teams to serve as an assistant editor. In this way, you will come in contact with hundreds of writers and you will have the opportunity to read their submissions critically and to choose the best one for publication. By comparing the all submitted articles, you will understand the differences between simple and excellent written manuscripts and then with the passage of time you will become a good editor as well.

Scientific blogging is **another way** to improve your writing and editing skills because for being a regular blogger you have to write and edit the contents regularly and after months of practice of blogging, your writing skills will increase gradually and it will make you a great writer and editor of scientific contents.

Along with magazines and blogging, **writing daily diaries** about your university life and happenings in your surrounding is also another way to improve your writing and editing skills. It is the practice of writing down your daily imaginations and feelings to handle and to understand them more clearly which leads to the improvement of your mental abilities also.

ISBN: 978-1-7779034-1-1

Studies have shown that those who have written diaries regularly during their university life, are good in finishing the given tasks and solving the surrounding issues as writing the incident and evaluating their causes have taught them to find the proper solutions easily and this could be the main secret of a successful professional life.

Another most important action or practice that can help you to improve your writing and editing skills is preparing a frequent report of every project assigned to you by a professor because preparing a report needs a comprehensive writing/editing practice and these activities are enough to polish your skills and enhance them to the expert level. For this purpose, you can start writing summaries of your weekly activities, you can write daily or weekly diary or even you can write abstracts to summarize your ideas etc.

You can also do your **daily blogging** about your university life and academic quests and can practice the communications and presentations as well. Along with blogging to present your writings, you can **participate in the workshops, seminars, and departmental journal clubs** which are the great platforms for students to learn how to present and evaluate.

ISBN: 978-1-7779034-1-1

Web Tools & Software Used in Writing

Writing a research article or starting a career in science and learning scientific writing is a passionate job for every student and early career researchers. Creativity and abilities to produce or correlate the pieces of knowledge are basic required skills to write a good research paper but along with all of these skills and abilities, familiarity with internet based web tools and software to ease the writing is vital to transform your simple research paper into a high impact research paper.

These web tools and software are classified into four sections which are further explained with examples in the next pages;

1. *Search engine/research tools to understand the current trends*
2. *Content enrichment tools to enhance the contents quality*
3. *Research formatting and content analysing tools to enhance presentation of an article*
4. *Publishing/content distribution platforms and social media tools to share or discuss your research*

ISBN: 978-1-7779034-1-1

Search Engine /Research Tools

Search engines or research tools are useful to understand the current trends and the keywords being searched around the world. Google, Yahoo or MSN are known as general search engines which are equipped with for-purpose and specific research tools. For example, google search engine is equipped with **Google DatasetSearch**, **GoogleTrends**, **GoogleScholar**, **Google Books NgramViewer** and **GoogleKeep** etc, which are important to understand what to write for scientific community?

SciSpace, **ScienceDirect** and **PubMed** etc are for-purpose and specific research tools that every researcher should know how to use for becoming a successful and impact full writer/author.

Content Enrichment Tools

Content enrichment is a process of simplifying the text, making it easy to understand and more useful for readers. Content enrichment is applied to enrich either the text or raw data to clean and clear. There are several paid content enrichment tools in market and **ContentMine** and **PharaseBank** are best free tools to use for the purpose of enrichment of your contents.

ISBN: 978-1-7779034-1-1

Research Formatting & Content Analysing Tools

Research formatting and citation analysis to arrange all (the text, tables, figures, conclusion etc) under a specific order as per journal guidelines is one of the most important phase of scientific writing where you are preparing the research paper for evaluation purpose so a journal can accept the article and publish it. Plagiarism is one of the common associated issue with all research articles and tools like **PlagiarismCheckers** or well-known **Turnitin** are very useful in this regard. **SciSpace** and **Citationsy** are very vital in reference management and along with **EndNote** and **Mendeley**, these all are what you need to format your research paper as per international standards.

BioRender, ImageJ and **Inkscape** are marvellous tools and software for developing or processing the images used in research work and make the research more attractive and easy to understand for editors, reviewers and readers. **MindtheGraph** is another wonderful and new web tool to create the beautiful graphic abstracts as the attractive graphic abstract increase the readership and citations more than five time than a paper with simple abstract. Basic expertise in using all these websites and tools will help you to write a wonderful scientific paper.

ISBN: 978-1-7779034-1-1

Publishing/Content Distribution Platforms and Social Media

When your scientific paper has been accepted and published by a journal and a **DOI** (digital object identifier) has been assigned, then you have to distribute your paper for global visibility and enhanced audience.

For this purpose, **ResearchGate**, **Academia** and **Mendeley** are very impact social media. You can also write the research news or story of your research achievement and can publish in **Academicinsight.ca** and **MyResearchNews.com** for improved citations and maximum global visibility of your research work.

- - - - - - - - - - - - - - - -

ISBN: 978-1-7779034-1-1

Chapter 3:

Pre-publishing Phase in Scientific Writing

Scientific writing is an integral part of the university life and a backbone of the academic career but when students or researchers are ready to publish a scientific article or a book, usually they don't consider the philosophy of publishing. The philosophy of publishing is described in the 5wh (What, Why, When, Where and Who) which is related and unique for every in-process scientific article or book. When a paper or a book is written based on the algorithm of 5wh, it becomes more attractive for the editors to enjoy the editing while reviewing the text and then for publishing managers to publish it proudly in their journals because these types of contents are valuable for the journals due to their potential impact in future.

Scientifically published contents (books, articles and patents) are valuable contents because these contents would be used as references by the scientific community to correlate their hypothesis or experimental results. In scientific or academic publishing, there are following three basic philosophical phases which should be considered carefully to create an impressive and impactful story.

1. ***Pre-publishing Phase***
2. ***In-press or Publishing Phase***
3. ***Post-publishing Phase***

ISBN: 978-1-7779034-1-1

Pre-publishing phase is described in the following 5wh sections of the scientific contents (articles, books etc);

1. *What to Publish?*
2. *Why to Publish?*
3. *When to Publish?*
4. *Who are contributors?*
5. *Where to Publish?*

What to publish? section is the most important section of a scientific article because it answers the basic question of what? It could be based on the data you obtained from experimental analysis or the context developed based on your vision but before the finalization of what to publish, select attractive keywords from google trends and other search engines as per following guidelines and use them in title, abstract etc.

1. Define discipline and sub-discipline of an article
2. List, download and read 50 highly scientific articles of the specified discipline
3. Select keywords for your article based on the comparative analysis of google trend and 50 highly scientific articles
4. Keep a regular analysis of keywords matching derived from sections 2 and 3
5. Search the finalized keywords in step 4 in research news and stories and use these keywords as the keywords of your scientific contents

ISBN: 978-1-7779034-1-1

Data derived from the experiments and visionary story developed in the brain are the explanations to justify **why to publish?** this research work. Try to focus on the significance of research work and include multidisciplinary aspect while explaining its application to improve life standards. Addition of facts and figures or diagrammatic explanation of the visionary story also can support the logic of why to publish?

After **what** or **why** are justified, then the most important thing is editing, proofreading and revision of the article to be ready for submission and to set the targets of **when to publish?** this research work. Timeline of the conception of story and preparation efforts for the first draft of the visionary story plays critical role in the writing and publishing of the paper or book because *time is wealth* and it keeps you on track of writing and completing the story. Data analysis, experimental revision, editing, proofreading and formatting are the associated but compulsory phenomenon of scientific coordination among research team members to reach the target. Time management acts as a chain connecting all players of research publication in a well organized fashion so when to publish is important to keep the water flow.

ISBN: 978-1-7779034-1-1

A scientific work is not an individualized work; it is always a team effort either it is in the form of scientific article/paper or a book. So building a team and deciding **who are contributors?** is the next section of your pre-publishing phase. These processes are dependent upon a very strong time management and clear picture of the outcomes of the research when it will be published in a reputable journal. A published paper or a book might have one or more authors but for sure there are many contributors who are contributing either as co-authors or editors or designers etc. Involvement of experts in all sections increase the professionalism in doing research work and also enhance the quality of publications which could be impactful in near future for being accepted in a journal and to receive thousands of readerships and hundreds of citations globally.

When you have found the answers of basic questions and know what are you going to share as a piece of knowledge with the community in the form of a scientific article and you know the timeline and your team then choosing a publishing platform is the last step in pre-publishing phase defined as **where to publish?** It should also be answered so that you can choose the right formats and themes for presenting your knowledge or scientific outputs.

ISBN: 978-1-7779034-1-1

Selection of a journal for your paper or a publisher for your book should be based on the global distribution potential or location or portfolio justifying that they have the potential or skills to show your research work to the world. If you are writing for the first time, then a start-up publishing group or an aspiring journal could be your best selection for where to publish your research work.

An experienced author who has published some books or scientific articles can also assist in choosing the right platform (publisher or journal) for publishing your first scientific work because doing mistakes and learning from mistakes instead of asking advice is a time consuming process.

'*Publication of your first scientific work is your lifetime memorable experience, make it worthy by choosing it wisely.*'

ISBN: 978-1-7779034-1-1

Chapter 4:

Scientific Articles & Types of Scientific Articles

Scientific publishing is not just writing an article and getting accepted in a journal or a platform where it has been uploaded. It is a complete set of procedures (SOPs) from idea conception to a defined target for each publication. It involves several publishing and post-publishing processes whereas writing and uploading the content on a publishing platform is only 1/5 of the total scientific publishing process. Scientific citations are the scientometric indicators of a scientific publication indicating the quality and how much valuable is the publication.

Scientific citations are the abbreviated alphanumeric expression embedded in the body of a scientific publications describing bibliographic references at the end of a publication for the purpose of acknowledging the scientific work. Scientific citations received by a research paper indicate how useful a scholarly article is rather than just a piece of useless knowledge. Scientific citations are important figures when research quality of an academic expert is evaluated because these figures tell us how the useful knowledge that scientist has produced as the productivity of science during his/her academic career. Journal citations are the referenced bibliography of the articles published in that journal as it tells the value of science published in the journal.

ISBN: 978-1-7779034-1-1

The impact factor (IF) or **journal impact factor (JIF)** of an academic journal is a measure reflecting the yearly average number of citations to recent articles published in that journal. This is worth mentioning that highest impact factor is 286 (2022) belongs to CA: A Cancer Journal for Clinicians published by American Cancer Society indicating the standards and professionalism in the presentation of science to the global community. Many young scientists focus on the number of publications in their scientific research career rather than the number of scientific citations. You can find several hundreds and thousands of young and early career scientists with 5-10-year experience who have published 25+ scientific articles but their citations are less than 100 because they ignored the most important part of their science career i.e. citations. The publishing process is not finished with the publishing of a scientific article but the real working starts after the publishing phase known as post-publishing phase where several actions are needed for the global visibility and improved citations. Post-publishing phase is aimed to distribute your research work which is fully explained in the next chapter.

ISBN: 978-1-7779034-1-1

To receive the higher citations for each of your article, you have to keep doing the post publishing processes for each of your scientific publication. For managing the balance of articles and citations, you have to understand several types of scientific papers and their vital components as variety of articles can result in the increased number of citations and increase the impact of your scientific profile. **Scientific articles** are the scholarly articles either peer-reviewed or non-peer reviewed written for the purpose of filling a gap in scientific knowledge or discussing views or opinions regarding a specific topic.

Writing a scientific paper helps you to understand how science works, and a good scientific paper helps the people to understand what real science is, so to create a mutual harmony and to connect the society with science, you have to focus on writing good scientific articles. Consider an example of a plant as your research work and a good scientific paper is like a flower on it producing fruits for the society.

A plant without fruit has no value for a society and currently, we are having jungles of useless plants indicating the necessity of good scientific articles.

ISBN: 978-1-7779034-1-1

Salient Features of a Good Scientific Paper

A good scientific paper should have the following salient features;

1. *Unique title and well informative abstract*
2. *Combination of multinational authors and contributors from academia and industry*
3. *Coherence and cohesion should exist in all headings and paragraphs*
4. *Continuous flow of knowledge is must among all sentences*
5. *Authentic and well cited references should be used in bibliographic section*
6. *Written precisely and concisely following the basic rules of writing i.e. no misspellings, effective and good grammar, free from first person pronouns and no-personal anecdotes or stories etc.*
7. *Should composed of the combination of effective words explaining the story.*

ISBN: 978-1-7779034-1-1

Qualitative presentation of an innovative story depends upon the effective word choice. Usually, researchers mixed the usage of words and verbs.

For example, mostly young and early career researchers don't know what is the difference between "examine" and "analyse"? (examine discusses the activities to gain knowledge whereas analyse discuss the analysis of gained knowledge). Following parameters should be applied for structuring the scientific article and enriching the text with effective words.

    i. *Knowledge*
    ii. *Comprehension*
    iii. *Application*
    iv. *Analysis*
    v. *Synthesis*
    vi. *Evaluation*

Scientific articles or papers could be 1) research or 2) non-research based on the work done or literature reviewed, respectively.

ISBN: 978-1-7779034-1-1

Scientific Research Articles are written to present a conclusion of series of lab experiments or data analysis. These could be the **original papers** if full set (more than three parameters of a scientific mechanism) of experiments have been performed or research note or **short communication** if focused on a single parameter of a scientific mechanism. **Case studies** are also considered research articles in every sector.

Scientific research papers are the written work presenting;

- interesting results

- innovative ideas

- critical discussion

- controversial conclusion etc

Scientific publishing platforms and journals are not a place of **storytelling**, so focus only *reporting the facts with references.*

ISBN: 978-1-7779034-1-1

A **scientific paper** is composed of following segments;

1. **Abstract** (summarizes why the research was conducted? how was it conducted? and what were the major results and conclusions?).

2. **Introduction** (should discuss what problem this research will address, why is this problem significant? How it applies to the larger field of research? All important concepts and terms should also be explained in introduction.

3. **Body** of the article (should address the set of experiments, models, or theories applied)

4. **Results** (should discuss the detailed analysis of the experiments, models, or theories applied in the body of the article supplemented with briefly explained figures and tables and graphs wherever necessary)

5. **Conclusion** and **Discussion** (is a section to discuss many points to be solved in further studies in the context of previous studies, discussing the problem, past and current attempts to solve the problem and the future perspectives clarifying the issue)

6. Some **acknowledgements** (a set of thanks for all kind of support received for the research work or drafting article)

7. **References** (primarily from research papers published in reputed journals, a small number of abstracts or textbook-type references (5%) and a few personal communications could also be included (5%).

8. **Tables and Figures** (high image quality, with minimal pixelization, should be referenced within the text of the article, usually in the results section. The figures and tables should be thoroughly described within the text, and their meaning discussed within the discussion section.

ISBN: 978-1-7779034-1-1

Multi-disciplinary Approaches in Scientific Research:

Writing a **research article** (original or short communication) for internationally reputable scholarly journals is a must to do job for all researchers and scientists. Scientists are putting their >90% efforts in lab work to generate experimentally validated data to publish a research paper because a good research paper is based on two things, experimentally validated data and a creative story behind it. These scientists are relying on data derived from science inside the lab forgetting the potential of data production by science outside the lab for their research papers. Data derived from multidisciplinary approaches enhances the reader's radar attracting audience from several disciplines and can receive higher citations.

Research articles in basic and applied sciences are mostly based on the tedious lab work consuming months even years along with huge money and human resources. Mostly data used in research papers is related to the structures, functions and interactions of molecules, chemicals, atoms etc. Most recently, big data approaches are being used in scientific research. Statistical data on public opinions is also a valuable tool in making scientific conclusions.

ISBN: 978-1-7779034-1-1

The whole science is not in the lab only, there is a big portion of **science outside the lab**. To explore the opportunities of doing research in science outside the lab, a researcher should apply multidisciplinary or even transdisciplinary approaches. For example, during the current Covid19 pandemic, serving the science and society is not just to look for vaccine development or diagnosing covid19. A researcher can study the social, psychological and economical impact, even political issues, public management, patient's behaviour, death rate, food habits etc could also be studied independently. International prestigious journals are looking for **novel stories** concluded based on the multidisciplinary approaches as these conclusions are presenting the ground facts.

Scientific non-research articles are concluded based on the already published literature of research or non-research papers. These are most comprehensive kind of scientific papers criticising a research methodology or protocols or giving opinions or suggestions regarding new methodologies based on the promising research work done. Review papers, commentaries, opinions, perspectives and scientific letters are few examples of such kind of research articles.

ISBN: 978-1-7779034-1-1

A **literature review** or literature reports are written to address a specific topic by evaluating research that others have done. A literature review is not a summary, and it is not a list also. The author cannot simply cite the studies that have been done and the results that have been obtained because a literature review should present a novel concept based on the critical analysis of already published research work. **Research articles** represent the work you have done whereas a **literature review** is the presentation of work done by others in your own hypothesis.

This is a challenging piece of work, so you must;

1. *Organize information to correlate your idea or research questions*
2. *Synthesize results into a summary of what is or isn't known or described*
3. *Identify contradictions, inconsistencies, and gaps in the research*
4. *Identify and analyse controversy when it appears in the literature*
5. *Develop questions for further research and give a new line of thinking to the researchers*
6. *Draw conclusions based on your evaluation of the studies performed by the community*

ISBN: 978-1-7779034-1-1

Writing a literature review based non-research scientific article should be based on your evaluation of the literature and of the issue at the stake. Before planning of writing a literature review, you should have read and analyse critically the related authentic literature (minimum 30-50 research papers and 10-20 review papers). You should evaluate the techniques applied, results obtained, conclusions drawn, and errors presented in each study, then apply your evaluation to the topic you want to write.

After the critical analysis, you should write a challenging, current interest, narrow, controversial or diverse topic of the review and write an abstract presenting your ideas or hypotheses containing brief summary of major studies investigated by the research communities.

You should answer following questions from the text you have collected during the review analysis of the research work;

ISBN: 978-1-7779034-1-1

1. What is the problem or issue being addressed? Is this problem relevant to my review?
2. Is the problem clearly stated? Is the significance of the problem discussed?
3. What are the strengths and limitations of the way the author has formulated the problem? Could the problem be approached more effectively from another perspective?
4. Is this paper primarily theoretical, experimental, interpretive, clinical? A combination? Could the study have been better if conducted in a different framework? (Propose a different and effective frame work and justify that with text and work done)
5. The theories to which the authors subscribe manifest themselves through their assumptions, interpretations, and conclusions. What assumptions have your authors made?
6. Has the author evaluated the literature relevant to the problem/issue?
7. How effective is the study's design? Is the method for investigating the problem appropriate? What errors does the method introduce? How accurate and valid are the measurements?
8. Are the conclusions based upon the data and analysis are valid?
9. Does this study contribute to our understanding of the problem? How is it useful to the community?
10. How does this study fit into my review?
11. How does this problem relates to the problem I will address?
12. How will I use or present the conclusions, methods?

ISBN: 978-1-7779034-1-1

Writing a Review Article for Scholarly Journals

Reading research papers and summarizing it – is a common trend in young researchers who are trying to write a scientific review paper and starting their research career with a passion but they face manuscript rejections by scholarly journals. The practice of writing a review paper is usually based on the bulk of knowledge researchers derived while doing study and this is the reason that more than 70% of review papers submitted to the scholarly and prestigious journals are rejected right after their first submission.

Summarizing the text while you are studying is for better understanding the science and you can have catalogued it for your better access whenever you are looking for a good reference but it does not mean that you can assemble this text under different headings and then submit it to the scholarly journals as a literature review paper. A Review paper is a novel statement or conclusion of a novel concept justified by the published research. You can also say that you have a better conclusion for the results published by other researchers and you are presenting your conclusion based on the results drawn by other researchers.

ISBN: 978-1-7779034-1-1

Questions While Writing a Literature Review

I.   Do I present a specific topic, problem, or research question? (Make sure you're not just summarizing a field of study!)

II.   Who is my audience? Will readers find my literature review relevant and useful?

III.   What is the scope of my review? What types of publications did I use (journals, books, popular media, government documents, personal communications etc?)

IV.   What am I reviewing? Is my issue addressing theory, methodology, policy, quantitative research, or qualitative research? A combination? Make sure this should be clear in your review paper.

V.   Has my search been broad enough to contain almost all the important and relevant studies?

VI.   Has my search been narrowed enough to exclude irrelevant studies?

VII.   Have I included enough sources? (Usually, anything less than a dozen sources is far too few for a literature review.)

VIII.   Is the literature I've chosen actually is relevant to my topic? Does every study I've chosen to include shed some light on the problem my article is addressing?

IX.   Have I critically analysed the studies or I just summarize the articles? Have I discussed the strengths and weaknesses of the studies?

X.   Have I cited and discussed studies that contradict my perspective or my hypotheses?

XI.   Is my review more than just a descriptive summary?

XII.   Is it organized into useful, informative sections that present different ideas revolving around my title?

ISBN: 978-1-7779034-1-1

Basic Components of a Literature Review

A short literature review is usually 7 to 10 pages long (single spaced). Most reviews, however, need to be longer to address all the material that needs to be discussed. Writing a good review is not about quantity, though – it's about quality. Weed out the unimportant and make your writing and logic tight under the following main headings;

1. **Introduction**: Introduce and discuss why this topic is significant. What will it discuss? outline the discussion order including a little background information and the discussion in next sections.
2. **Body**: The body of your review article depends upon your topic. For example, if your topic discusses and evaluates three different methodologies, you might divide the body of the article into three sections, each discussing one of the methods. In these sections, be sure to describe and evaluate the studies in detail, comparing them and discussing their implications.
3. **Discussion and Conclusions**: You should conclude your review by novel statement and a fruitful purpose of the article rather then discussing the conclusions you have made. You should also discuss the implications of your study and what are the perspectives?
4. **References**: Literature reviews published in reputable journals usually cite 75 to 100 studies. A short literature review usually requires less than 50.

ISBN: 978-1-7779034-1-1

Things Not to Do While Reading Research Literature

1. Downloading too many papers at a time for reading
2. Copy pasting the text from papers
3. Putting too much time on a single paper
4. Ignoring the figures and tables of a paper
5. Searching the author profiles and their other works

Things to Do While Writing a Review Paper

1. Critical thinking all the time
2. Avoid making general conclusions
3. Summarize results and analyse data instead of summarizing text
4. Keep discussing specific conclusions with your research fellows
5. Keep searching related industrial outputs

Writing a review paper needs critical reading skills and skills to analyse the published data and making predictions regarding a probability of results. Reading few hundred papers, extracting the text and re-writing to avoid computer based plagiarism will not make you a good researcher or scientist. A good scientist or a good researcher is always thinking critical issues and find possible solutions with minimum harm to nature. Simply it can be concluded that it's all about brain game and creativity to write a good piece of science.

ISBN: 978-1-7779034-1-1

Advantages of Writing a Review Article

Students and young researchers during master or PhD study and research work in university, focus only to enhance their lab working skills due to several reasons but in fact they are focusing to be a good technician instead of being a good researcher because expertise in lab work produce good technician whereas expertise in understanding the research can make you a good researcher. These young researchers work to produce good results so that they can publish their first research article and they do not pay any attention to write a (non-research) review article which has potential following advantages;

1. *It enhances your critical thinking and writing skills*
2. *Writing a review paper helps you to understand what is happening around the world in your research discipline*
3. *It improves your data analysis and conclusion making skills*
4. *It helps you to increase your total citations and h-index*
5. *It opens up new windows in research career such as editing, writing, analysing etc.*

ISBN: 978-1-7779034-1-1

Writing a review paper is a tedious but most important and a must learn job for a researcher because these are the review papers which guide us that either the research in specific discipline is moving in right directions or the current methodologies are sufficient enough to reach the desired goals in a specific discipline. It is a fact that a review paper requires huge set of knowledge but keep it in mind it is not a collection of literature review. A review paper is a non-research scientific article presenting a novel point of view or conclusion from the research done around the world. As it has been described earlier, it is the a new conclusion of the past research done and justification of several results to have a new conclusion.

For example, in covid19 case, you can study all the published clinical reports and correlate the efficacy of covid19 vaccine in reducing mortality and can present your point of view regarding public vaccination programs and can suggest good alternatives with solid logics and references. You can also correlate the multi-disciplinary articles published in health sector to reach a conclusion of pandemic management and its economic, social or political impact on the laws and policies of a state.

ISBN: 978-1-7779034-1-1

Types of Scientific Non-Research Articles:

There is a common misconception that to publish a scientific paper, a person should have done some kind of lab work and you can publish a scientific article only if you have amazing results but in fact there is a several kind of scientific papers which do not require any kind of lab work. These kind of papers could be published if you have skills of creating novel stories and making conclusion of published work. Following are 10 famous known types of these kind of scientific papers;

1. *Technology Development Report (TDR): A Scientific Article for Start Ups and Innovation Corporations*
2. *Scientific Meeting / Conference Reports: Summarizing the Scientific Activities*
3. *Case Reports (Clinical/Technological / Academic/Organizational etc)*
4. *Scientific Opinions / Commentaries / Perspectives: The Science of Mind and Prediction*
5. *Statistical/Epidemiological Reports: Reporting the Facts and Figures*
6. *Hypothesis or Scientific Ideas*
7. *Scientific Letters / Letters to the Editor*

ISBN: 978-1-7779034-1-1

Technology Development Report (TDR): A Scientific Article for Start Ups and Innovation Corporations

Transformation of science into a product or service is the best way of serving the society because commercialization of these technological products makes life better and brings wealth in the community. This developed technology is patented usually before commercialization and can be explained well in technology development report describing all aspects not mentioned in patent file so that readers can have a broader vision and understanding on the developed technology.

Technological development is the phenomena of transformation of a scientific knowledge into an applicable process which can solve a part of social problems and can improve the lives. Technological development and its commercialization process is a scientific transformational protocol required by the industry to develop a usable product or service and sell in the market. Technological Development Reports or TDRs are the step-by-step explanation of the overall process to explain the series of events involve in the development of a technology from the invention to the diffusion in the society or respective industry.

ISBN: 978-1-7779034-1-1

Technology Development Report is the best category indicating the applied research happening in the technology zones around the world. Every researcher doing applied research or every techno-entrepreneur/chief technology officer developing a start-up based on an innovative technology can write a technology development report explaining the innovation, feasibility, commercialization model, significance and future perspectives to gain the customers and partners from all over the world.

Technology development report is an important scientific article explaining the integrity of scientific, industrial and management disciplines. The authors of these reports are extraordinary talents in their field and could be the one or more of the following;

1. *Applied Researchers or Principle Investigators*
2. *Technologist / Technology Development Officers*
3. *Start-up Founders or Co-founders*
4. *Chief Technology Officers (CTOs)*
5. *Commercialization Experts of Technology Departments*
6. *Government Employees working in Science and Technology Divisions*

ISBN: 978-1-7779034-1-1

Components of Technology Development Report (TDR):

A technology development report is a mechanistic explanation of a technology developmental process explaining how a technology is developed in academia and applied in industry. A technology report should have following important components…

1. **Introduction**: What type of technology is being developed?
2. **Historical Background**: What are the roots of current technology?
3. **Invention & Innovation (Patents etc):** Why is it different?
4. **Feasibility (Economic, Operational or Scheduled):** It should mention the inputs and outputs of every section of feasibility.
5. **Models (Current & Past):** List the brands or models using the current technology or commercialized based on the current technology.
6. **Significance (Why has it been developed):** Statistics and figures on the producers and consumers
7. **Perspective:** What would it be in the near future?
8. **Developer's Comment or Message**: A general conclusion and discussion

ISBN: 978-1-7779034-1-1

Scientific Meeting/ Conference Reports: Summarizing the Scientific Activities

Reports are always informative and assist decision making groups to develop suitable policies. Scientific meetings/conferences are vital components of research ecosystems where thousands of same discipline researchers gather and present their latest findings.

Writing a report on a scientific meeting/conference is to summarize these findings and making a strong critical analysis which would help the community to create a new dimension in research and other researchers will also get to know what is happening around them. Scientific meetings and conferences are integral part of research ecosystem where the researchers present their promising results.

Every institute or research lab is doing the research with a different vision and perspective but these scientific meetings and conferences are magnets to attract all these researches to create a new dimension. Panel discussions of almost every meeting/conference help to reach a common point of view of doing research in a better way.

ISBN: 978-1-7779034-1-1

Writing a scientific meeting/conference report is as simple as to understand the raining process but all it needs is attention and smartness to do critical analysis and making conclusions. Suppose hundreds of researchers are presenting their research findings which are not related to each other but all having same purpose indicating that research is not moving in the right direction. So skills of making conclusions and defining dimensions is necessary to write a meeting/conference report. Writing a scientific meeting/conference report having interesting and trending conclusion can help the science journals, news media groups and young researchers to understand what is happening in the relevant research field. These reports can also act as catalyst for industrial cooperation because business experts may have low understanding of science but they are expert of analytical conclusions. Publishing the scientific meeting/conference report is the last task after making a strong conclusion from the discussions and presentations in a meeting/conference. After drafting the meeting/conference report, submit it to the relevant scientific society journal, national journal or journals publishing commentaries. List of speakers can also be studied as one of these speakers could be the editor of a scholarly journal and will have interest to edit and publish the report.

ISBN: 978-1-7779034-1-1

Components of Scientific Meeting / Conference Report:

A Scientific Meeting/Conference Report is a critical analysis based on the hundreds of presented research in an annual meeting of a scientific society or reputable national/international conference. A Scientific Meeting/Conference Report should have following important components...

1. *Introduction*
2. *Geographical Significance of Research*
3. *Sections of Scientific Meetings/Conference*
4. *Critical Analysis of Presented Research*
5. *Conclusion*

Writing scientific meeting/conference reports can have a potential of receiving hundreds of citations as these are the extracts of hundreds of research groups having valuable information. For example, these reports have the information of research activities of all these research groups so all those groups can also cite this report in their introduction or discussion sections of their scientific articles describing the presentation way of the potential of their research work for the benefits of the society.

ISBN: 978-1-7779034-1-1

Case Reports (Clinical / Technological / Academic / Organizational etc): The Critiques for Comparative Studies

Case reports are well known part of the academic writings because these reports describe extra-ordinary or a distinct incidence happened in a patient's behaviour, institutional achievement, technological development or a case report on a cutting edge innovation in an organization. Currently, the well-known case reports are clinical case reports whereas other types of case reports are technological (advancement/distinction) case reports, academic or organizational specific case reports describing innovations or distinct achievements.

Clinical Case Reports / Case Reports in Medicine are comprehensive explanation of symptoms, treatment status, disease follow up or a surgical situation of a patient. These are the most common types of case reports published by scholarly journals as almost every clinical researcher is publishing one or two case reports/year. A non-clinical researcher can also visit the clinics or hospitals and with the coordination of authorities, can search for an extra-ordinary behaviour and can write a clinical case report using inter-disciplinary quantitative research approaches.

ISBN: 978-1-7779034-1-1

Technology boom is a current trend all over the world and every day we are witnessing the awesome technologies coming in the market. Some technologies are market attractive whereas some technologies are not being welcomed by the people, so researchers can write case reports on technological boom explaining the social, economical and political factors in the success or failure of new technologies. Every technology officer can also write technology case reports explaining the distinct features of their technologies with others.

Almost all progressive institutes or organizations including universities, colleges, research groups, NGOs, private corporations or national/international committees perform several innovative activities throughout the year and achieve distinctions among others. A member of these institutes or organizations can write an institutional or organization case report or an outsider can also write a comparative case report describing the impact of specific organizational model on their achievements and distinctions.

Writing a case report is a rare phenomenon among non-clinical researchers because institutes or organizations have not defined these categories for their incentive programs. Although top scientific non-medical journals have not included these types of publications in their scope but there are many inter-disciplinary and general science journals accepting creative stories focusing a specific issue. A case report could be highly productive and impactful scientific publication criticising the global trend of ongoing research and helpful to determine the right direction for experts.

ISBN: 978-1-7779034-1-1

Main Components of a Case Report:

A Case Report is a critical analysis and collection of facts on a specific topic featuring a distinguished behaviour, achievement, development or innovation related to a disease, academic institute, technological group or an organization, respectively. These reports could be known as Clinical Case Reports, Technological Case Reports, Institutional or organizational case reports etc.

A **Case Report** should have the following important components;

1. *Introduction of **Topic** & **Problem***
2. *What is **Distinct** in this Report?*
3. *Social Impact of the **Distinction***
4. ***Inter/multi-disciplinary** Relationship*
5. *Critical **Conclusion** & **Perspective***

ISBN: 978-1-7779034-1-1

Scientific Opinions / Commentaries / Perspectives: The Science of Mind and Prediction

Science is the knowledge derived from a research methodology based on hypothesis and assumptions. These hypothesis or assumptions are based on some observations but a scientist or researcher having expertise in a field and history of doing research can present valuable opinions and commentaries. These opinions/commentaries are extracts of decades of analysing the scientific conclusions and can help young researchers defining their scientific targets.

Scientists and researchers are walking libraries and they are having knowledge of thousands of research work done around the world in a specific sub-discipline. They are well aware about the mechanistic approaches being used in the research and their possible outcomes because these scientists have spent decades of doing research and managing hundreds of graduates and post-graduate students. After studying the thousands of research works on a specific topic, an experienced researcher or a well known scientist can give wonderful and useful opinions for science managers, publishers and emerging young researchers who are ready to take a deep dive into the ocean of scientific explorations.

ISBN: 978-1-7779034-1-1

Scientific opinions & commentaries are the conclusive remarks of senior professors, eminent scientists and team leaders predicting the future or future-way of the research. These are written by the well-known researchers, eminent scientists or experienced professors. Scientific opinions could be about research methodologies, science policy, institutional behaviour or the dealings of early-career researchers. Young researchers can also write scientific opinions or commentaries describing the challenges, issues and barriers being faced in their research careers. Young research can also write scientific opinions or commentaries as narrations of their senior professors, eminent scientists and well known researchers.

Scientific opinions are valuable thoughts based on the thousands of research works happened whereas scientific commentaries are valuable additions or explanations of an ongoing research topic to improve the methodologies and strategies for better outcomes. Scientific perspectives are predictions of a scientific methodologies, approaches or technological development of an issue based on the decades of research mostly are written by the noble prize winners and winners of international prestigious awards all over the world.

ISBN: 978-1-7779034-1-1

Main Components of Scientific Opinions or Commentaries:

Scientific Opinions / Commentaries or Perspectives should have following important segments;

1. *Proper explanation of research history*
2. *Proper usage of scientific terminologies*
3. *Well-presentation of issues and challenges (when written by early-career researchers)*
4. *Predictions or outcomes of applied research methodologies or strategies*
5. *An understandable and logical conclusion.*

Scientific Opinions, Commentaries or Perspectives are to help the coming generations to understand the applications of research methodologies and defining their targets. These kind of scientific articles are to fasten the scientific development because young researchers work in right directions with the most suitable approaches instead of wasting time and resources to learn from the experimental mistakes. These act like accessories of scientific knowledge based on the valuable comments of eminent scientists discovering the unknown.

ISBN: 978-1-7779034-1-1

Statistical/Epidemiological Reports: Reporting the Facts and Figures

Statistical/Epidemiological reports analyse the numerical data to describe an objective in the form of graphs, charts, tables, etc. These reports provide useful information for managers to identify the problems and take proper actions. Statistical reports have broad applications especially in clinical research, which are well known as epidemiological reports.

In an epidemiological report, scientists use statistical analysis to describe a health phenomenon in a numerical way. The main goal of these kind of reports are discussing the spread of a disease and underlying risk factors and prevention or control strategies for a specific or general group of individuals. To reach the real target of these reports, a multidisciplinary scientific team must derive data from several scientific disciplines, such as biostatistics, informatics, biology, economy, social, behavioural sciences etc.

When you write an epidemiological report, in the first step you have to notify the distribution i.e frequency and pattern of phenomenon. **Frequency** mean the number of phenomenon (mostly health events) in a specific population comparing to the total population.

ISBN: 978-1-7779034-1-1

The best example of frequency in COVID-19 epidemiological report is the number of infected cases and their relationship to the total size of population. **Pattern** in epidemiological reports defines specific template for the health phenomenon based on time, place and persons under study. You have to explain a time pattern for a disease you are studying, which could be daily, seasonal or even annual. In addition, many health issues are geographic specific phenomenon so you should differentiate **populations under study** such as school, city, state, country and the world as epidemiological report are community-based studies. Differentiating the geographical sections with community segments is very critical in making the conclusions. For example, regarding persons under study, you have to consider variations such as age, behaviours, socioeconomic issues, environmental exposures etc.

The last important step in writing an epidemiological report is **searching for determinants**. Determinants means any factor and causes effecting health conditions or other characteristic. In another words, you have to find the relationship of progression of disease with different potential risk factors.

ISBN: 978-1-7779034-1-1

Epidemiological reports are used to measure the frequency of a disease and potential risk factors associated with that disease in the groups of individuals. Therefore, these kind of reports are the best approaches for determining the causes associated with health-related conditions in a society.

Estimating incidence or mortality of a disease within specific population can provide clues for preventing and controlling the diseases. Getting information of the disease pattern is main step of writing a scientific paper by biomedical scientists who are involved in the discovering of the pathways of diseases or introducing a highest level efficient treatment. Identification of a region or population with higher rate of disease and all variables effecting its incidence, may provide a comprehensive perspective of the disease for the scientists.

Thus, epidemiological reports are powerful tools for biomedical scientists and clinicians to define the target lines and border lines of their studies. In addition, statistics or actuarial science is the basic of every epidemiological or statistical report and the data of actuarial science is a vital player for every scientist to make a productive and fruitful conclusion.

ISBN: 978-1-7779034-1-1

Main Components of Statistical/Epidemiological Reports:

Statistical/Epidemiological Reports should have following important segments;

1. *Historical back ground describing the purpose/s of current report*
2. *Demographical analysis and value of specific demographic*
3. *Past and Current case status (or cases under observations)*
4. *Statistical methodologies applied to study the facts and figures*
5. *A productive conclusion*
6. *A future perspective of the study*

Along with biomedical scientists and clinicians, policy makers and leaders are also looking for epidemiological reports to plane the strategies of managing diseases and saving millions of lives. Political leaders read these reports easier than a paper containing lots of scientific terminology. Therefore, any epidemiological or statistical report in a specific region will be viewed and cited by those who are decision authorities in the related discipline.

ISBN: 978-1-7779034-1-1

Scientific Hypothesis or Ideas: Justifying the Imaginative Power in Science

Science is the published knowledge developed after the series of justified experiments or statistical analysis and this is also true that for publishing a scientific article, you don't need to perform several experiments, invest money and time and then reach a conclusion to publish it. Scientific hypothesis or ideas are specific types of scientific papers and very few journals publish these after a proper editorial and peer-review. These hypothesis or ideas are valuable for the scientific communities because they give the targets to the research communities to think in a different or an alternative way to find the solutions of an issue.

If you have a strong knowledge about a discipline and have read thousands of research work based scientific papers about a topic and have an idea that by changing strategies or applied in another way can improve the research results so based on the justifications or logics from the published authentic research work as strong references, you can supporting your hypothesis or idea and can publish it in very rare but reputable journals. To understand the concepts of scientific hypotheses or ideas, you have to study several hypotheses published by that journal before starting the hypothesis or idea.

ISBN: 978-1-7779034-1-1

Main Components of Scientific Hypotheses or Ideas:

Scientific hypotheses or ideas are rarely described scientific papers and they don't follow a specific pattern because each journal publish these in entirely different formats and these are mostly non-peer reviewed scientific papers. The basic purpose of such kind of scientific papers is to support the scientific communities with innovative ideas or destination defining hypotheses pointing the wrong way chosen for experiments. Following important sections could be useful to draft a scientific hypothesis or idea which should be edited and formatted for the specific journal as per journal requirement;

1- *Historical background of the issue and attempts to solve the issue*

2- *Validated points to disapprove the currently applied experimental approaches*

3- *Statistical evidences justifying the need of innovative hypotheses and strategies*

4- *Possible risks associated with the novel proposed approaches*

5- *A future perspective and conclusion*

ISBN: 978-1-7779034-1-1

Scientific Letters / Letters to the Editor

Scientific letters or letters to the editor are regular types of scientific papers (either peer-reviewed or non-peer reviewed) which could be research work base or literature search or either could be discussing a perspective or an opinion. Almost every journal is publishing these kind of letters which are being sent by their regular readers or authors discussing the policy or types of research being published etc. These are the same letters to the editor published by general magazines or newspapers but these scientific letters are unlike to the newspapers and are pieces of science following all scientific methodologies rather than just a criticism or opinion.

Mostly these letters are describing a controversial result or a tentative statement about a methodology and are composed of all important components of a research paper or a review paper but these letters are without sections and headings. These are having referenced or pictorial justification of the statements made in each sentence. Sometimes researchers who want to just present a one specific result of their research rather than a discussing the complete set of experiments, they write letters to the editors.

ISBN: 978-1-7779034-1-1

Chapter 5:

Standardization and Common Mistakes in Scientific Writing

Scientific articles are the integral part of a scientific career and a good scientific article (either a research work based scientific article or non-research work scientific article based on the literature review) should follow some standardization rules to increase the quality and authenticity of the article. Several common mistakes could be made by researchers, especially by the early career researchers while drafting their scientific articles. Following are the few standardization tips and common mistakes to improve the each part of a scientific article;

1.   Abstract (250-350 words)

Why is an abstract important? Readers use the Abstract to decide whether they want to read the rest of a paper or not. It must contain enough information for them to understand the work, and for them to decide whether it applies to their research project, interest or not. The reader should be left with no doubt about what was the purpose of this study? what were the methods used? what were the major results? and why are those results important? The rest of the paper will fill in the details. A good abstract should be **Succinct, Clear, Balanced** and most importantly **Focused**.

ISBN: 978-1-7779034-1-1

Normally, **abstract consists of 7-8** sentences.

- **Sentence 1-2:** Investigation and explanation of the problem.
- **Sentence 3:** Aim and Objective of the study that why this study has been done?
- **Sentence 4-5:** Summarization of the important methods used to investigate the problem.
- **Sentence 6:** Summarization of major results - not *all* of the results
- **Sentence 7:** Interpretations of the results.
- **Sentence 8:** What do you suggest to convert your results into scientific law?

The Abstract **should NOT** contain:

- Lengthy background information - that belongs in the introduction
- Lengthy materials and methodologies - that belong in the Methods section
- References to other literature
- Abbreviations or acronyms
- Figures, images, or references to them

ISBN: 978-1-7779034-1-1

Standards in Reviewing the Abstracts

Criteria to judge Abstracts. Different journals use different standards, but these cover the basics

1. Author states **why** was the research conducted
2. Author states **how** was the research conducted
3. Author states **what** were the major *results*
4. Author states **what** were his/her *conclusions*

Structuring Abstract

The abstract should follows the "Problem - Purpose of this study -Methods - Results – Conclusions'' sections.

Common Mistakes in an Abstract

1. Abstract like an introduction.
2. Most of the abstracts lack purpose of study and justification of results.
3. Sometime justification contains too much information which creates negative impact of study.
4. Abstracts are not very concise and precise.
5. Non relevancy of the information.

ISBN: 978-1-7779034-1-1

2. Introduction:

Standards to Review Introduction

1. Background information
2. Previous studies described
3. Statement of the problem
4. Motivation for this research
5. Significance of this research
6. Presentation of hypothesis

Common Mistakes in Introduction

1. Too much and non-specified information is presented to increase the text
2. Unclear what study is and confusing structure
3. Flow of knowledge is not observed in the introduction section, it seems all sentences are first copy pasted and then edited
4. Manuscript should not contain first-person anecdotes such as I found, my research etc.
5. Minimum one sentence of each standard of introduction has been written presenting the understandable statements

ISBN: 978-1-7779034-1-1

3. Methods & Materials

Standards to Review Methods & Materials

1. Materials (Enough and Relevant)
2. Methods (Enough and Relevant)
3. Controls (Appropriate Negative and Positive Controls)
4. Experimental approach (Adequate to Test a Hypothesis).
5. Flow chart or diagrammatic explanations of experimental approach worth a lot.

Common Mistakes in a Methods & Materials Section

1. Too much and non-specified information.
2. Background/Introduction material included for example, this is ok: "Samples were prepared using the method described by Newton et al. (2000)" - but this is not: "This theory was first proposed by Newton et al. (2000)."
3. Explanation of methods applied by other researchers.
4. Reporting results and discussions.

ISBN: 978-1-7779034-1-1

4. The Results Section

Standards to Review Results

1. Results exposition (Sufficient and appropriate detail for well presentation)
2. Experimentation/number of trials (Sufficient to Test the hypothesis)
3. Believable data and appropriate statistical analysis

Common Mistakes in a Results Section

1. Raw Data
2. Redundancy
3. Discussion and interpretation
4. No figures or tables (every section should have at least one table or figure)
5. Repetition of methods/materials reported
6. Presentation of all results obtained in the lab
7. Comparison of results with the work of other researchers
8. References are given

ISBN: 978-1-7779034-1-1

5. The Discussion Section

Review Standards for Discussion Section

1. Motivation for study (clearly restated)
2. Interpretation of results (sufficient and logical)
3. Possible limitations and sources of error (adequate discussion and acceptable errors or challenges)
4. Ramifications (clear and realistic)
5. Very strong correlations

Common Mistakes in Discussion Section

1. Introductory explanation
2. Irrelevant discussion
3. Combined with results
4. New results
5. Broad statements (only appropriate even for major, ground breaking papers)
6. Ambiguous data sources and confusing results in conclusion
7. Self-created statements found
8. No conclusive statement found

ISBN: 978-1-7779034-1-1

6. Tables and Figures:

1. High resolution
2. Have neat, legible labels
3. Clearly formatted
4. Indicate error and give detailed captions

Note: Captions are one of the most important elements of a good manuscript.

Review Standards for Figures & Tables:

1. Figures & tables are properly constructed as JPEG images (i.e., they are not constructed in word, they are not saved as power point files, they are saved as regular JPEG image files).
2. Figures & tables are properly numbered (Figure 1, Figure 2, Table 1, Table 2)
3. Visually and textually clear: Figures and graphs are clearly labelled
4. Choice of figures enhances understanding of the text
5. The captions are detailed and thorough
6. The figures and tables can stand alone without the rest of the article

ISBN: 978-1-7779034-1-1

Common Mistakes in Figures & Tables

1. Inappropriate Format
2. Redundant Information
3. Ugly
4. No Caption
5. One-Liner
6. Regurgitates Figure/Table

7. References

Review Standards for References

1. Uniform
2. Old, new and self-studies
3. Citation in text and arrangement in bibliographic format

Common Mistakes in References

1. Formatting
2. Type of Reference

ISBN: 978-1-7779034-1-1

Useful Tips While Writing a Scientific Article

Writing a scientific article is a skilled job and it is not a very fast learning skill, it is based on the passion to write and create novel scientific sorties. Following useful tips can help you to improve your manuscript;

1. Avoid too much information, be very specific
2. Don't mix up sections, create good linkage among them
3. Make conclusion very clear, precise and concise
4. Review papers are not short books or book chapters
5. Write very unique title with well informative abstract
6. Avoid scientific misconducts i.e. authorship gifts, redundant publication
7. Protect contents from writing frauds such as plagiarism etc.

ISBN: 978-1-7779034-1-1

Chapter 6:
Post-publishing Phase in Scientific Writing

A scientific article is not just a published article, but an article that will be read and cited. For an article to be read and cited well, you need to do comprehensive and repetitive post-publishing processes.

A very good scientific article that can receive thousands of read and hundreds of citations, should have following characteristics defined by **Prof. Robert Houze,** from the **University of Washington.**

> *'Make sure the abstract, introduction, and conclusions touch all the same points. There should be a one-to-one correspondence between the points made in each. One useful idea is to use a highlighter to mark the points made in the abstract, intro, and conclusions to make sure there is closure.'*

It should be noted that there are 65+ million scientific papers have been published in indexed journals which have received 1500+ million indexed citations till now indicating the direct relationship of a paper with the citations it received after the publishing. These articles can receive higher citations only in case if these are distributed properly using several approaches. Some of these approaches are discussed in this chapter.

ISBN: 978-1-7779034-1-1

Scientific papers are the written work presenting interesting results, innovative ideas, critical discussion, controversial conclusion etc. As per statistics published by international agencies, there is an average 25 citations per document published globally and if you have published paper in your portfolio which have not received 25+ citations, then a strong post-publishing services for that paper is required.

Geographical distribution of average citations by each country is given in figure below for your consideration;

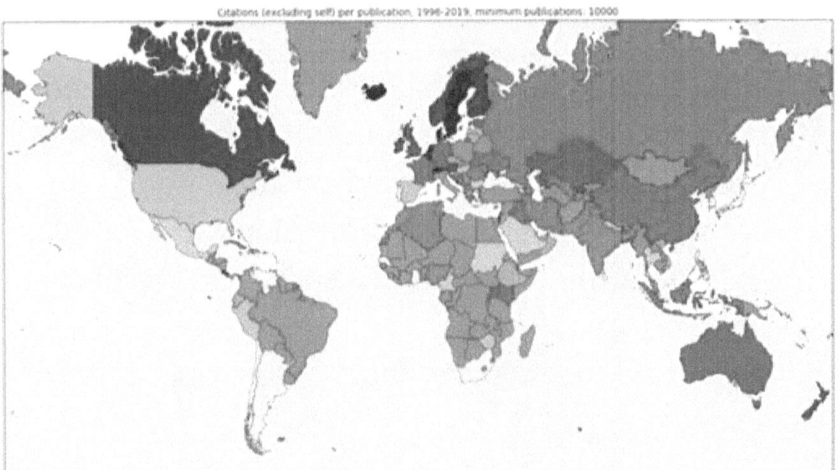

ISBN: 978-1-7779034-1-1

Scientific Citations and Post-publishing Strategies:

Scientific citations give proper credit to the authors for the words or ideas that have been incorporated into your paper. Post-publishing process account for more than 30% of a journal management job with the targets of paper distribution for global visibility and increased citations. Mostly journals management team have post-publishing departments and they do the post-publishing process to enhance the global visibility of the articles they are publishing but as an author, you can independently follow the post-publishing strategies to increase citations of your articles. There are several effective strategies are applied for post-publishing process, following four are more important;

1. **PaperShare** (1-personal & influenced social media, 2-conferences and seminars, science special social media like Academia, ResearchGate etc)
2. **Affiliateship** (1- professional national, international and local societies, researcher networks)
3. **Science blogging** (research news and research stories)
4. **Encyclopaedia addition** & eBooks publishing

ISBN: 978-1-7779034-1-1

PaperShare

Your published research paper is a valuable piece of knowledge because it has passed several review process and is now accepted by the scientific community as an authentic research work. It gets its value when it has a broader audience and for this purpose almost all researchers share their papers but pasting the abstract page on the research groups notice boards in a tradition way. Sharing your paper just among the members of research group who you are working with them is not enough, you have to use all the strategies of PaperShare to increase the readership of your research paper.

Of course you share your research paper on your personal social media pages but you should contact the influenced social media pages where you think they have scientific audience and request to share your paper on their pages. They might charge a fee for this but to increase the readership, you have to pay these fees.

You also have to join the scientific social media such as Academia, ResearchGate and share your paper on these pages. Regularly participate in scientific conferences, seminars and journal clubs to share your paper and discuss the related research to increase the technical readership of your research paper.

ISBN: 978-1-7779034-1-1

Affiliateship

Being affiliated with societies, associations or networks is another way to increase the readership and citations of your published research work. Scientific societies or associations are usually the learnt societies composed of the researchers and scientists. These societies could be at university level and could be societies of students or early career researchers.

There are national scientific societies on every subject in almost every country, sometimes these societies are mandated by the governmental authorities and in some regions these are acting as NGOs. Every national level society is a member of an international society or international federation composed of national societies from almost all countries of the world. These societies offer memberships on annual of lifetime bases in several categories such as full membership or student or early career memberships with a small amount of fee and these are great platforms where you can create an audience of your research work and also you can learn from the reputable scientists in specific disciplines. Researcher networks at an academic level or on internet are also good platforms to join for increasing the global visibility of your research work.

ISBN: 978-1-7779034-1-1

Science Blogging

Science has been developed by the scientists to resolve the issues of society. Every segment of developed science is highly beneficial which is being used and applied by the general public. There have been an anti-science mind-set for centuries due to its intersectional nature with other disciplines of philosophy but scientific communications can create a bridge between the general public and scientists. Science blogging is a process of providing the authentic scientific information to the general public, early career researchers and the people who are interested in the science.

Scientific journalism is an integrated part of science mostly ignored by majority of the global scientific communities which is well known because of the publication of research news and stories. **Writing the research news and stories** is an important part of science puzzle as it is the only way of spreading knowledge to the general public to connect society with science. It is also a way of global visibility for your published research because research news and stories create social engagement and reach the global audience which are containing the links of your full text access.

ISBN: 978-1-7779034-1-1

Research news are not like the abstracts you published with your research but it is the correlated conclusions of your research well-written in simple language. It can have attractive title unlike the research papers and also it can have non-referenced text for making research more interesting to be read by the broader audience.

Research news usually have a text of minimum 500 words with or without references but most importantly, these texts should have trending keywords in title / body and easy-to-understand literature to breakout on the internet and should be published on research news blog after you publish your research. Don't forget that your research news is not for high level researchers but it is for the undergraduate students or scientific readers with a population of over 100 of millions.

Writing the Research News & Stories

Writing research news and stories is a post-publishing process which are necessary for distributing the published research and to have more global visibility of published research. When it comes to write a research news or a story, it is important to know the ABC of all basic tools and software before writing the scientific contents.

ISBN: 978-1-7779034-1-1

These web tools and software are classified into three section;

1. Google tools to understand the current trend
2. Content enrichment tools to enhance content quality
3. Publishing platform such as science/academic magazines and research news websites to publish your research news i.e MYResearchNews.com, AcademicInsight.ca etc
4. Social media tools to share your research news and stories.

First of all, you should know the **'GoogleTrends'** because it tells us what is being searched around the world and what topics we should choose for writing along with the **'GoogleScholar'** which tells what types of articles are highly cited at all time. Create an interesting title of 11-13 words derived from Google Trends/Google Scholars as these are the focusing keywords of your news.

Then summarize your research in a paragraph of maximum 250 words using the simplest and easy-to-understand words and finally write a paragraph of maximum 200 words describing the role of your research in our daily life.

ISBN: 978-1-7779034-1-1

Don't forget to visit the **'ResearchGate'**, **'Academia'** and **'Mendeley'** on regular basis to understand what is being discussed most among scientific communities as these platforms will help you to elaborate the potential of your research work to improve the social lives.

After summarizing the basic theme of your research news, improve and enrich your text using **'ContentMine'** and **'PharaseBank'.** These tools also help you to improve the content quality you are going to publish.

At the end, always cross check your text using **'PlagiarismCheckers i.e. Turnitin etc'** to avoid possible copyright and plagiarism issue.

You can publish your research news at **'MyResearchNews.com'** when it is ready for publication.

Personalized research news blogging is the only way to win social support regarding the research you are doing. Scientific blogging creates social engagement of a larger audience on a specific topic which tells you when, why and what has to be published in scientific communities.

ISBN: 978-1-7779034-1-1

Encyclopaedia & General Readership

When we publish the science (i.e. scientific papers) we have a special scientific audience (students, researchers, academic experts etc) who are reading scientific papers and noting few of the papers for using as citations to their own work. The scientific paper is a valuable article if it has big audience and high citations it has received. Most of the researchers ignore to reach the general audience which is a part of the post-publishing process to increase the readership of their article. General readership is important for creating the value to the scientific paper but mostly the general audience is not having interest in the reading of scientific articles. This general audience is reading the science from encyclopaedias and books on regular basis so to increase the reach of general audience to your research work, you have to work on how to add your papers to the encyclopaedia articles or books which are published for general readers related to your discipline. For this purpose, you can search the related articles on Wikipedia and edit these articles to increase the interest or can create new interesting articles on Wikipedia while citing your work and giving the value to your research. For example, see the picture on the next page;

ISBN: 978-1-7779034-1-1

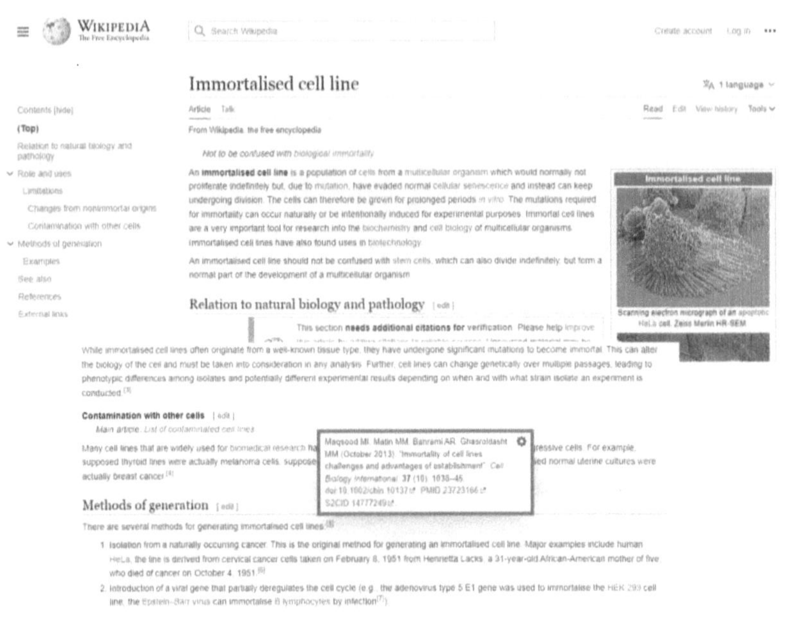

You can also publish eBooks discussing the significance of your research via creative stories because many of these general readers are aspiring researchers and in this way they will found your research valuable in near future. For publishing eBooks, self-publishing platforms such as Kindle Amazon, Apple iBooks, Kobo, Nook, Scribd etc are the great choices. You can visit the website of each platform and read the guidelines for authors. You can also read a sample book entitled **'Genes and Cells for Skin Diseases** – *ISBN: 978-1-7779034-4-2'* available on Amazon Kindle.

Chapter 7:

Writing/Editing as a Profession and Challenging Career

Scientific publishing represents the technological advancement of a society as it indicates the productivity of scientists living in that society. Suppose, if about ten thousand (10,000+) scientific articles are being published from a society of 1 million, it indicates that 1% members of the society are learnt scientists and these learnt scientists along with the technology development, innovation and commercialization experts ensure the sustainable development of a society following the United Nation's sustainable development goals (SDGs).

Scientific or academic writing/editing is a multidisciplinary career of integrative skills and knowledge. To step into this career, an individual should have the complete basic knowledge of all sciences, engineering and technologies. History of publishing scientific articles with good impact and good citations increases the chances of success. As it is a multidisciplinary career, basic knowledge of ICT, software engineering and technology development is must for maintaining the creativity and innovation in this career. Don't forget that this career comes under the category of Media and Communications domain, so you must know the current rising trends in the global publishing industry.

ISBN: 978-1-7779034-1-1

To start a career in the scientific writing/editing/publishing, the most preferred way for early career individuals to be a part of a research project you can be a published co-author or self-publishing in case of books. For career in self-publishing, good business management, entrepreneurship development and digital marketing skills ensure the success. Writing/editing/publishing career does not mean you are writing for others and publishing your written work with their names, but write and publish for yourself. You can also provide editing and publishing consultancy services to others (individuals or organizations) when you have gain much expertise and have built a good portfolio as scientific author or editor.

Writing/editing is a noble profession where you are surrounded by creative stories either written by you or edited by you. It is a highly impactful profession where you can rule over the minds of millions and billions of readers around the world with your unique contents. You can play vital role in the cultural development of a society because a writer or editor can preserve the myths, traditions, customs and history of a region or ethnic via creating interesting and long lasting stories in the form of articles, magazines or books.

ISBN: 978-1-7779034-1-1

A writer is always writing and creating new stories whereas an editor has a job to revise and improve the written contents of aspiring writers/authors. An editor may be following responsibilities while working professionally;

1. *Revising/editing contents for major technical issues*
2. *Revising/editing stories to maintain knowledge flow, syntax, and grammar etc*
3. *Reviewing the contents and supporting writers to improve their drafts*
4. *Evaluate proposals from writers and develop ideas for enhancing creativity*
5. *Networking among writers and other players of publishing industry*
6. *Analyse the budget and negotiate for contracts*
7. *Coordinate authors to ensure on-time publication of contents*
8. *Format the contents and writing style as per journals/books publishing platforms*
9. *Prepare the KPIs (key performing indexes) and track the published work*
10. *Study the reader's mind-sets and establish a strong opinion in publishing sector*

ISBN: 978-1-7779034-1-1

Specialized Skills Required for Being a Successful Editor;

An editor is not a person born with tons of knowledge and skills but a person who understands the logics and flow in nature. **Creativity and curiosity** is considering as most valuable talent required for being an editor because as an editor you have to revise and upgrade creative stories every day. An editor should know how the **knowledge flows** in written contents and is conveying the hidden message, clearly.

An editor has the ability to improve the contents so it could be more **impressive and flawless**. An editor should have very **strong critical reading**, writing and **communication skills** because an editor is connecting the beads of readers, writers, publishers in a productive string of knowledge.

An editor is doing most valuable job of **polishing and preserving the science, culture and ideas** in the form of contents and texts. **Experience in knowledge management** is the only way to enhance the set of skills required to be a successful editor.

ISBN: 978-1-7779034-1-1

Following 10 are **most valuable skills** required for being a **good editor**;

1. Knowledge of grammar and article structure
2. Skills of creating stories from raw concepts and ideas
3. Strong communication and interpersonal skills
4. Organizational & time management skills
5. Project management and brainstorming skills
6. Creativity and curiosity
7. Rapid adaptability of ecosystems of entirely different mind-sets
8. Skills to finish the projects on time and work efficiently under pressure
9. Basic computer skills such as word processing software and internet surfing
10. The ability to spend time alone and relax mind when required

ISBN: 978-1-7779034-1-1

Writing/editing is a profession of creating long lasting social and cultural impact in the form of wonderful and interesting stories but it is not all. A writer/editor could be a player of game changing in politics at national and international level because expertise in this profession is the expertise of reading minds and playing with it. It also creates a strong economic impact by creating a revenue stream not just only by selling the books or papers but in the internationalization of local brands and attracting the audience form the globe, the reason content is known as the king of business. **Writing/editing** can also create academic impact to enhance productivity of an academic/scientific institute to attract the international funding and students from regional countries and enhancing the international academic collaborations.

So, you are going to start writing after completing this book and with the passage of time, you are going to be an excellent writer and editor. As an excellent writer and editor, you are going to be a part of the game of changing the impact and perspective about the society you are living in or a topic or discipline you are working on. So I can say all of you a simple sentence...

Welcome to the game!

ISBN: 978-1-7779034-1-1

About The Author

Dr. M. Irfan-maqsood, PhD, is an independent researcher at IMAQ Research Ltd and scientific editor at IMAQPRESS where he has been editing to improve the quality of contents and developing several content management systems. He has received five universities degrees/diplomas, all from the world top 1000 internationally ranked universities.

1- BSc (Biology/Chemistry),

2- MSc (Molecular Biology and Biotechnology),

3- MA (Political Sciences – International Relations),

4- PGD (Entrepreneurship Development) and

5- PhD (Cell and Molecular Biology),

He has introduced the concepts of pre-publishing and post-publishing in developing world and has been awarded three time as a national innovative tech-preneur focusing on the development of research and knowledge-based start up and established IMAQ Publishing Pvt ltd which later on has been budded off as IMAQ Research, IMAQPRESS and IMAQ Technologies Ltd in several countries. As an independent researcher, he has published 3 books, edited 4000+ text contents and 26 scientific articles in reputable journals which have received about 500 citations, globally.

ISBN: 978-1-7779034-1-1

Other Books By This Author

MAGA – The Untold Legend
(MAGA & MAYA)
(ISBN: 978-1-7779034-0-4)

MAGA is the founder of Magan Civilization established thousands of years ago in the mid of Asia connecting two land segments of three continents Eurasia and Africa and ruled the whole ancient world for thousands of years. This story explains the MAGA from Zindia - the planet of eternals, as a bearer of super powers who ruled the 99% of old world and created all ancient civilizations except Mayan Civilization which was founded by his own twin sister MAYA, another Zindian on earth.

I am a Failed Entrepreneur: A Story of Experiences and Challenges
(ISBN: 9-781777-9034-5-9)

'I am a Failed Entrepreneur' is not the story of failure of Dr. Irfan-maqsood, because there is no failure in entrepreneurship. It is the story of failure of his first start-up company launched in Iran due to several challenges. The chapters of the book, 'I am a failed entrepreneur', has explained characteristics of an entrepreneur, entrepreneurship lifestyle and achievements an entrepreneur can have on his/her early phase of entrepreneurship journey. It also explained the personal experiences and all challenges on this road an entrepreneur can face and how to deal the challenges in an efficient way.

ISBN: 978-1-7779034-1-1

This page intentionally left blank

ISBN: 978-1-7779034-1-1